See the Divine Light

PETER HENRIK ERTNER

SEE THE DIVINE LIGHT

Forlag: BoD · Books on Demand GmbH, In de Tarpen 42,
22848 Norderstedt, Tyskland
Tryk: Libri Plureos GmbH, Friedensalle 273,
22763 Hamborg, Tyskland
ISBN: 978-87-4304-173-3

Stop for a moment and sit down, visualize that your heart opens, pray to whatever God, Guru, person, or even an object as one have confidence in, as a symbol and a representative for a higher being for showing one extraordinary, limitless, blissfully, miraculous, direct opening to the Divine Light.

The following pages is a personal testimony and an inspiration to whoever who could imagine this, as a worth of trying.

Seing the Divine Light is not a particular -Buddhist- experience.

No one is empowered or owns the right, to teach this practice in any ways.

This is a universal possibility, that is shining inside every single living being under the surface, only waiting to realize itself through a direct meditative experience.

Nevertheless, it's only an opportunity which is within range for human living beings.

About the topic for whom is empowered, or who has the right to teach these different meditations tools for seeing the divine light, is correct in some way if it's in some special aspect of Buddha, for one will be practicing, because it maybe is tantric and therefore an empowerment from a teacher in a direct line from Buddha.

Therefore, one will make a connection to this teacher after the initiation to the practice, this teacher do not own it but have the heavenly authority to pass it on to others.

It is important to find one's root guru fast, because it is said it can be dangerous to jump around from guru to guru and into different spiritual systems. A great teacher once said to me, " If you choose to fly one meter with one airplane and one meter with another airplane you will never reach the other side".

The human body is a very precious vessel for our soul / mind, therefore, working with these tools, which is revealed here and in a certain extend simply illuminated from another angle, my angle, nothing new in this text will appear for when it comes to the goal as described here. The interesting part is that any person from the west can do the exact same as a person from the east when it comes to spiritual development.

It will be more precious than gold because it will if succeeded be a part of oneself into eternity.

Buddha has said that if one opens up and realizes the nature of one's mind, which is an unlimited joyful white golden shining light via one of the chakras one will no longer be reborn in the 3 lower realms inside the wheel of life.

These 3 incarnations are categorized as Hell, spirit/ghost or animal.

So, what is this light?

It's the true nature of one's mind, and actually also for every living being waiting since eternity to get discovered through endless lives efforts and now when one has collected tremendous good karma, makes one understand the importance to make this journey for the benefit of all sentence living beings.

This light is a very real and incomprehensible powerful experience, sitting in meditation with my eyes widely open calling the buddha aspect from my heart radiating though my 3 eye the Light manifested right in front of me filling the whole room up with a brilliant golden shining light like a golden sun radiating heavenly beautiful blissful lights to all sides of the room for a relatively long time, about 10 to 15 minutes. After that it melted into me as an explosion of joy and in that moment the realization became a reality.

After some hours of meditation in highest joy, under a razor-sharp clear vision awareness and a fantastic felling of unlimited space, it slowly faded away.

The mind recognized itself and mirrored itself directly.

The light in the room would not have been possible for another person to see.

To put the things in perspective, after one have opened up that inner door, metaphorically, one have placed one'self in a fast car driving on a straight illuminated highway leaving the dark forest behind and are now driving directly connected towards the holy spirit as is in one's own mind.

After this experience one do not need a guru or Lama anymore, the divine light is the meditation focus until one will reach the full enlightenment.

That also means one's prayers for something or anything if not there are a karmic block to the specific situation etc., then prayers will be heard much more proactive than before.

It is a very big turning point in one's spiritual perception after this has happened.

For me it still took years from that point of actually see the divine light until I got my full consciously realization implemented in my perception of myself, when that happened I felt more grounded and stronger.

So when have such approach setting the mind up to do all this effort for others and not just oneself prevents the exercise to become belly bottom focused.

It's also essential to build up more merit good karmic imprints and to avoiding building up ego because setting up mind towards the benefit of others will be a good antidote against ego.

Or there is a risk one can develop spiritual materialism.

An example is before I were rich, beautiful, intelligent, have a lot of spiritual artifacts around me and on me, and now I am also a spiritual individual.

So, the ego must not grow.

So, to get higher wisdom then need to build up more good karma, then and eventually get a higher understanding of one's self and the existence itself.

Wisdom has to be balanced with love and compassion, wisdom is to see things how they are without any disturbing veils within oneself, love and compassion without wisdom is not good.

As a human living being we are here in this relative and dualistic world to understand that the other side of all relative phenomena is the absolute existence or the true reality of one's own mind that is the cosmology of Vajrayana Buddhism.

The relative world and the absolute world is two sides of the same coin.

That is so beautiful because one does not have to look long away or far away in the universe the salvation is direct in front and inside oneself.

The center of the universe is right where one sits.

The understanding and a direct experience of the emptiness of all relative phenomena will also give realization because emptiness is inseparable from realization or the true nature of mind.

It's not empty as there are nothing, minds emptiness is limitless joy, space, wisdom, love and compassion and shinning divine light, so these feelings are absolute feelings.

There are some Buddhist sayings.

Emptiness are joy, joy are emptiness, joy and emptiness are inseparable.

Space is information, information are space, space and information are inseparable.

Form is emptiness, emptiness is form, form and emptiness is inseparable, or relative is absolute and absolute is relative is also inseparable.

Doing this exercise even for beginners with no spiritual experience is not dangerous.

It's not easy to know which spiritual level or potential one has before starting up with meditation.

For me it took approx. 2 years from when I first was introduced to Vajrayana Buddhism also known as Tibetan Buddhism meditation in the age of 19 from a spiritual friend to the realization of my mind when I were 21.

It simply happened in my apartment where I lived and had as a base for my life and job and social activities, so it is not a must to retreat in the Himalayas in a cave or in a Lama monastery.

Even though I have participated in many short retreats and visits in the Himalayas, Kathmandu, India, and many different places in Europe later on, it's my conclusion that it's better to do it in Denmark or in one's resident country.

So, it does not have to be very exotic surroundings to make the meditation practice.

It's important to be aware that the understanding of one's realization have to be fully implemented in one's own perception, that means that after the direct experience where one realizes one's minds nature it can take years before its fully implemented with in one's awareness of oneself.

When that happens, one knows it very clear, and one will proclaim it to others if needed even when one is highly realized but a fully enlightened person will never proclaim one is fully enlightened even if the person know he or she is it according Buddha.

I want to emphasize that I do not have the ability to see which realization level a person is on just by looking or see or hear the person.

No matter what, always have a critical sense towards and when approaching a spiritual teacher.

A famous female translator once told me about all this with the persons who have the title Rinpoche, these times there are gone an inflation in that title so that means one shall not get intimidated but be critical and open.

There are in my knowledge very few fully living enlightened individuals.

Guru Rinpoche, also named Padmasambhava is considered as the second historical Buddha have said that it is easier for females to break through to the awakening state of mind than males.

The Realization is not the same as the Enlightenment such as being a Buddha or an awakened one, the realization is the first step out of 10 steps until one achieves the tens level and becomes a Buddha a completely awakened individual understanding the deepest meaning of the existence and full understanding of emtiness and also not getting more incarnations inside the wheel of life.

On the 1 to 9 level one can and will make mistakes in life, and one will still be under the influence of karma in all of its aspects, its only on 10 level the person is said not to be under influence of karma anymore.

But let's focus on the first and most important level.

I want to clarify, that this book is for all people, written by a western person with no traditional Lama education.

The definition of a Lama or having the title of Lama, require that the person has followed a 3.33-year supervised meditation retreat a recognized place or have gotten a real intellectually Lama education over many years.

If not have one of these one is not a Lama but is of course not excluded to be or to work as a meditation teacher within the same branch as a Lama, but not to fall into semantic I just want to clarify that a good teacher does not have to be either Lama or similar does not need to have a title as Lama or Rinpoche for the matter, just have to be able to awake one's ability to start meditate and inspire.

Looking for a Lama, meditation teacher, Guru, spiritual friend, is a very serious matter in terms of finding the right one for oneself.

After finding Guru etc. and starting up with Guru, one can do own practice and do not need Guru anymore later on, one knows oneself what to do and how to develop.

To say it, I recommend trying to speed up the meditation skills as fast as possible because going a traditional way is in my opinion very boring and intellectually complicated and it is not necessary when it comes to the goal that this book strive for.

Example, a student from the Gelug Buddhist tradition, that is from the school where His Holiness Dalai Lama is the holder they study for 28 years before starting op meditation.

Of course, it's very individual from person to person, what is best for oneself, monk, nun, Lama, layman/woman, or the Yogi way, but in general, we in the west do not need all that intellectual knowledge or as I will describe it, too much intellectually noise, block oneself to see the forest for bare trees.

If one tends to get lost in details or cannot relate to meditation without a very detailed explanation and a super exactly visualization of the meditation delivered of a person in red orange clothes with a high intellectual title, one is not ready for the individual Yogi way where it's all about getting spiritual results, more than knowing Buddhas teachings into detail's but to feel the energy inside oneself and be more sensitive, the goal is the full awakening by any means.

With the Conscious direct Realization of one's mind which is the first Buddha level and especially from the 6 buddha level and ahead special abilities and powers appears within oneself.

On the 6 level one will get illusory transparent rainbow light body.

And example of this is a real life story of a Austrian woman being in cave retreat in high and cold Himalaya for 25 years alone only doing 1 meditation called Thumo, inner fire, as she reach the realization through that meditation alone with nearly no intellectual knowledge about Buddhism before she started her retreat under supervision of a master as a young woman in the Himalayas.

That is of course very difficult to do this way of practice and not many can do that, myself too but again it's not necessary to reach realization to do these incredible hardships upon oneself.

Thumo is the ability to keep warm under extreme cold environments, it's 1 out of 6 doctrines where also the super important pratice Phowa is one of them developed of the Buddha Yogi Naropa from India about 1000 years ago.

My own way is the Yogi way.

Starting up meditation with the awakening awareness of the importance to go this way for the benefit of all living beings is the most important self-understanding discovery a person can get, and also within the Vajrayana Bodhisattva Buddhist way.

It's not possible to obtain higher levels of realization without this mindset but it is possible to reach the first level without it.

Furthermore, living a normal life with job etc. should not after my experience be affected negatively in terms of view to meditation or more important, after one have "seeing the light ", but I will admit that many things changed and I lost many friends in that period of my life.

Seing the light is a revelation a personal opening up to a whole new dimension in one's mind.

It does not directly give one neither less or more materiel prosperity it has nothing to do with that.

Prosperity materializes from good karma.

Karma is cause and effect.

An another very good ability is to have a strong faith and be a strong believer because under meditation the awareness has to be clear and concentrated towards focus point.

To get more faith accumulated in one's mind simply just need build up more merit and good karma.

This can be done by physical actions or by different meditations techniques.

One technique is called Give and Take.

One visualize sending out heeling light when breath out via nose and take in dark sufferings from others when breath in, it goes to the heart where it transform into light, can do this naturally for few minutes every day.

Another technic is to visualize one'self become unlimitless physical big filing the whole universe and then just let emotions and thoughts drift past not use any of it as a reference point let it drift by like clouds on the sky, that can relax the mind.

That is of course not done overnight but through the startup of meditation, prayers, visualizing the best for others, different offerings, blessings and help from spiritual friends etc. then one eventually, become strong believer.

To be a strong believer is the key word in meditation, believing is very important, actually it's not possible to develop without it.

Strong fate is the key that opens up the door into heavens realm.

But if use meditation only to get a calmer and more focused mind to help one in life and on job it can also be a merit build up tricker even if one do not do it to be more spiritual.

About Karma, which is a very complicated theme to get around with, because building up good karma can if the influence of lack of wisdom is dominating one's judgment, the acts just do the upper sit of good karma, but if one's actions is done with a pure motivation the bad karma is less bad, or maybe not bad at all, it depends on many factors, if the acts are done under influence of the disturbing emotion called ignorance, bad karma is accumulated even though if one do with good intentions.

What a wonderful thing just hiding there inside oneself.

Even though meditation is just a practice where one sits down and visualizes different things, saying different things etc. then it actually can be a potentially overwhelming experience, and the divine light is so an incredible mind explosion of joy so it's actually beyond words to apprehend the experience.

My own life up to the aged of 21 have been to optimize my

performance as a elite sportsman, I have both achieved to be national champion in Olympic weight lifting and I have done full triathlon Ironmans.

But heading for the enlightenment is the ultimate goal in my opinion.

Even though there are little physical in meditation, mind is over matter and one can build on different exercises to one's practices and benefit from that, it's not advisable to copy a Tibetan persons physical life because they down prioritizing all physical things unless its body prostrating, also personal I do not have much confidence in Tibetan traditional medicine, we have here much better possibilities to live healthy and comfortable and benefit from the spiritual tools they have kept alive for 1000 years and now slidely vanishing in Tibet but arising in the vest.

I do also practice macrobiotic yin yang vegetarian lifestyle, no smoking or drinking the most of my life too but it is not a must if practicing Vajrayana Buddhism, but it is advisable if one have the strength to live that way because it help discipline the mind.

Also, any consumption or intake of consciousness expanding substances and drugs is an absolutely no go within this the highest form of Buddhism, Vajrayana.

My root Guru is a Tibetan Lama, Venereble Tenga Rinpoche, I meet him from the beginning of my spiritual journey also upon many I meet from the beginning the Great Danish teacher Ole Nydahl, I have several personally spiritual wonderful moments with him, one was with sacred Gau on my head blessing, which turned into a thing called hook into ring, as means I opened up and connected into the same energy universe as from where his blessing is channeled from, It send me into another mental state of mind where I were completely aware and blessed a very powerful and short but concentrated moment, another funny thing is I asked him how he bless others and I got his secret to actually do that as he initiated and empowered me.

I can say that within the perspective of world Vajrayana Buddhism, it is historical what Mr. Nydahl and his wife has accomplished in terms of spreading the Dharma, but I am not a personal follower of his lineage called Diamond-way Buddhism as he is the personal founder of, but Mr. Nydahl is when it comes to meditation and as a person a very competent charismatic person to be close to for a startup practicing person, but of course when this words are made this possibility to meet him when he was in his prime are long over, I feel lucky to have been close to him many times before also several days in the place in Malaga where it where only few persons there at that place.

Mr. Nydahl has among others a very significant ability to transmit and project powerful blissful energy into a person.

He is also competent to teach in one of Naropas six doctrines called Phowa, a practice all people should use a week of their life to complete its a very important meditation only need to do it one time.

The holder of Phowa is a Tibetan Lama called Ayang Rinpoche.

Its advisable to use the Vajrayana Buddhism tools to reflect over the emptiness of all relative phenomena because it will be a help under meditation and in general in terms of one's perception of fear.

Fear when practicing is destructive, and it will block for progress.

Dealing with fear is an essential theme.

Vahrayana Buddhism or Dharma as it is called, means how things are.

Originally it of course came from the historical Buddha from India 2500 years ago, but it was very limited of whom got that teachings, it was first in large scale put out into practice from the second Buddha Guru Rinpoche also known as Padmasambhawa who also came from India and brought it to Tibet more than 1000 years ago.

There is something called ` post meditation ´, and meaning by that is, after sitting meditation and reflection on things emptiness, then after the sessions meditation just jump over to be an alert and aware state of mind of everything in and around oneself in the daily life trying to be in a constant flow of awareness.

So, meditation

After progression when wisdom starts to show itself after months or years within one's perception of reality, fear then fade away giving more room for one's inner warrior taking steps into the big unknown universe of one's mind.

Om Tare Tuttare Ture Soha

This is a Mantra of the female wishful-filling compassionate green nonphysical all present buddha as one can pray to, because this divine energy is said to be very present in our physically world of today, its therefore beneficial to recite this mantra many times.

So there are many mindsets one can do when heading for this incredible experience as the realization, because my conviction is that stressed out people want to find a deeper meaning in their life but off course not want to abandon a good life with job activities family etc. because that is not necessary to do.

I will emphasize that if one see Buddha as an ordinary person one will get an ordinary persons transmission, but if one with great critical sense and great openness towards the teacher no matter if it's a Buddha or not one will get the highest transmission, it goes also in the state of meditation.

Buddha or no one can make a person into a realized or awakened being one must self-turn the stone's, the teacher can only guide and bless the student.

So I come around many topics and try here ending up collecting lose ends towards the goal to see the divine light, I will try not to make this a intellectual Buddhist story because if one is very intellectual one could end up being a nihilistic person and that's a shame but not all bad because someone have to keep the teachings authentic, Buddhas full gathered teachings is filling a whole book university full of teachings.

There are 2 worlds within Buddhism, intellectuals vs yogis.

No matter how complexed and advanced and difficult

intellectual a subject is it is just one big illusion, it is completely emptiness.

All phenomenon are projections of the mind.

I came around a radio program where they told that scientist have found out that time probably did not exist at all.

That is not correct time do exist, but only on a relative level, our relative world and our self do exist relative, but absolute it does not exist.

When one meditate on all relative appearances as empty the divine light at some stage when one is ready appears in front of oneself.